THE GROWER

seeds

Grow your own cut flowers from scratch

MILLI PROUST

Photography by Éva Németh

Hardie Grant

QUADRILLE

To Jan Wansell,
thank you for your kindness and encouragement;
without it, the books might not be

contents

introduction

Nothing represents the promise of life and all the beauty it can hold than seeds. Encased in a little protective shell, seeds contain the blueprint of potential. They are tiny vessels of hope that hold the secrets of growth, adaptation and the perpetuation of life. Each and every seed is a testament to the indomitable spirit of nature and the planet's intrinsic drive for renewal. When it comes to growing and tending, I am both an observer and active participant – the beauty of the plants draws us in, and as I plant their seeds in the soil, sheltering them from the worst of the weather and protecting them from marauding predators, I become the caretaker in this life-giving cycle.

Working in our gardens fosters a sense of purpose, mindfulness and gratitude for the beauty that surrounds us. Our acts of cultivation, nurturing tiny seedlings and witnessing their full transformation into beautiful flowers, not only connect us to the cycle, they remind us of our own capacity for growth, resilience and renewal. With a packet of seeds, life can become as beautiful as you want to make it.

Milli x

"A seed contains everything it needs to begin a life as a little plant."

soil
essentials

Celebrating the humble earthworm

soil essentials

Creating a flourishing cut-flower garden with abundant blooms begins with the soil. To achieve the best results, it is important to pay attention to the type and structure of your soil, as well as its PH level and the climate in your area.

Understanding the workings of soil and its impact on plant growth can make the journey of sowing seeds and troubleshooting much easier. Therefore, I encourage you to read up a little about soil before beginning your gardening endeavours. Basically, don't skip this first bit – it's important!

soil layers

Soil is made up of layers, also known as 'horizons'. There's the ground surface, the topsoil, the subsoil and the bedrock.

Most plants will grow in the topsoil only, but it's worth exploring how deep the topsoil on your site is and what lies beneath it.

For example, if your subsoil below the topsoil has been compacted in the past from machinery or a particularly wet climate, it will affect the overall drainage of your growing plot and it will likely flood during heavy rainfall, even if you're blessed with lovely, free-draining topsoil.

topsoil

The more organic matter in your topsoil, the darker it will look. Topsoil varies depending on the soil type (see page 10).

- *Contains most of the ground nutrients and fertility; most plants will grow here*
- *Will usually be 10–15 cm (4–6 in) deep*
- *Most soil micro-organisms, insects and worms usually inhabit topsoil*

subsoil

Usually lighter in colour than topsoil and generally has a mixture of silt, sand and clay in it.

- *Supports the topsoil*
- *Contains fewer microbes than topsoil*
- *Absorbs and holds on to some of the water and nutrients that trickle down from above; also provides minerals*
- *Anchors taller trees and deep-rooted plants, which can then access the stored water and nutrients*

bedrock

Bedrock can extend kilometres deep into the Earth. Through natural processes such as an earthquake or erosion, a piece of bedrock can be exposed to the surface, and to the elements like wind and rain. This process allows it to be broken down, restarting the soil-making process. You can also see bedrock in outcrops in places like mountaintops, man-made quarries and along rocky coastlines.

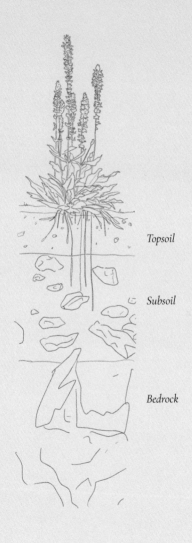

Topsoil

Subsoil

Bedrock

soil types

Get to know your soil. Certain plants will thrive in different soil conditions and fail in others. It's far easier to work with your soil type in your plant choices than to battle against it; your garden will be healthier and happier for it and growing will be much less hard work.

Take a handful of your topsoil, add a little water and roll it in your hands until it is the size of a golf-ball. Observe it. Squeeze it between your fingers and see how well it holds together. Rub some between your fingertips to get a sense of the particle size.

chalk

Chalk soil has big particles and is often stony, free-draining and alkaline. The topsoil depth will vary before hitting solid chalk. Shallow chalk soil is prone to drought and is low in nutrients. Deep chalk can hold moisture better and, therefore, can be home to a larger variety of plants. If you are growing on chalk, choose plants that will thrive in an alkaline environment.

sand

A sandy soil has gritty, solid particles, with no pockets to hold onto moisture, so it is very free-draining. It accepts water well but finds it hard to hold onto. It warms and dries quickly, and finds it hard to retain nutrients, but has plenty of aeration and oxygen.

silt

Silt soil is very fertile, but true silt soil is very rare. Usually found near a river, it has a slippery, soapy texture. The fine particles can become compacted easily. Because they can be carried by water, they can easily be washed away.

loam

Loam is soil with a good balance of sand, clay and silt (usually mainly sand and silt, with a smaller amount of clay). Loam soil is crumbly, free-draining, and water- and nutrient-retentive, making it perfect for growing a vast variety of plants. Loam will hold its shape when squeezed but will crumble when squeezed hard.

clay

Clay is sticky and smooth, and rolls into a firm ball that won't be broken apart easily. Clay is made up of tiny particles, making it drain much more slowly. It stays cold for longer, holding back growth in early spring. It holds on to moisture and nutrients very well, but may have not-so-good drainage and hold less oxygen for the plants.

soil pH

The pH level of your soil can have a significant impact on the growth of different plants. The pH level determines which nutrients are soluble in your soil and, therefore, available to plants, which can affect their ability to thrive. For instance, ericaceous plants are known as 'acid lovers' and may struggle to grow in soil with lime, an alkaline substance. However, most plants do well in soil with a pH between 6.0 to 7.0, which is considered neutral. Don't worry if your soil isn't neutral though, because many plants have adapted to thrive in more acidic or alkaline environments.

To determine the pH level of your soil, you can observe the kind of plants that grow in your area and identify the type of soil you have. However, to get an accurate reading, you can send a sample of your soil for analysis or use an easy-to-use home testing kit.

Once you know your pH, play to your strengths and choose plants, that will live happily in your soil – this is particularly important when planting perennials, trees and shrubs, which have longer lives than annuals. Annuals, as a general rule, will be slightly more tolerant of your soil conditions.

healthy soil and healthy plants

Soil needs to provide oxygen, water and nutrients to your plants. The better your topsoil is at providing these three things, the healthier and happier your garden will grow.

If you're experiencing plant health issues, it's advisable to test your soil before turning to chemical solutions. If your plants are struggling to grow, are showing a yellowing in their leaves and are not productive with their flowers your soil may be lacking in nutrients.

However, excessive dryness, wetness, acidity or alkalinity can all affect how different plants take up nutrients too.

There are numerous options available, including simple at-home kits, for analysing soil samples, which can help you identify if nutritional deficiencies are causing stunted growth. These tests can also provide information on the pH level of your soil.

improving your soil

The single best thing to do for your soil health and structure is to add a mulch layer of the highest quality, organic compost every year.

HOW TO MAKE COMPOST

There are just four main ingredients to a thriving compost heap:

GREEN MATERIAL *such as vegetable or fruit scraps, grass clippings, flowers, fresh leaves, seaweed, and fresh animal manure.*

BROWN MATERIAL *such as dry leaves, cardboard, newspaper, wood chip, sawdust, straw, dried grasses, woody stems, chopped twigs, eggshells, and wood ash.*

OXYGEN *the oxygen can reach the heap by adding a little chunky material in with the brown, such as bits of twigs or chunks from woodier stalks such as shrubs, amaranths and artichokes. These may take longer to break down, but it's OK to have a few lumps left in the compost after it's cooked.*

WATER *the compost-making material should be moist – not leaking water, but damp like a wrung-out sponge. There will already be a lot of water present in the green materials added, so I only water my heap when it's drying out. Water can knock out oxygen, so it's important not to over-water.*

Dahlias on the compost heap; the centre of the heap turns to compost

FOR THE BEST RESULTS:

- Aim for approximately 60 per cent green material and 40 per cent brown material in your heap.
- The simplest way to measure the split is by layering: add a layer of green waste to the heap followed by a layer of brown waste and so forth.

- Monitor the mix – too much green (nitrogen) and the heap will turn sludgy and stinky, too much brown (carbon) and the heap will take a really long time to decompose.
- Amend your ratios accordingly.

heat in your heap

If your compost heap has everything it needs, it will get hot.

You don't need heat for the composting process to happen but it will help speed up the breakdown process.

The heat comes from the bacteria multiplying. If you can turn the pile, allowing oxygen to reach the middle, it should get hotter – this only needs to be done once, if at all. Mixing it all up will boost the parts of the heap that are not performing so well, raising the overall temperature of the whole heap.

The heat is useful for killing off weed seeds, so you can even throw weeds onto your heap without worry. The core of the heap is the hottest part, so if measuring, measure the temperature from there. The temperature will naturally rise and fall depending on the bacteria.

You don't want it to get too hot (71°C/160°F), or it will start to kill the good bacteria and halt the decomposition. Aim for 32–65°C (90–150°F).

Comfrey is incredibly nutrient-dense, particularly high in potassium (which encourages lots of blooms, and in turn fruit to set), so add it to the compost heap and it will act like manure.

YOU WILL NEED:
Comfrey leaves
A bucket
Rock or a brick
Water
A makeshift lid for the bucket

1. Pack the comfrey leaves tightly at the bottom of a bucket or container. Weigh them down with a rock or brick. Fill the bucket with water and cover. Let it 'brew' for about three weeks.

2. When ready to feed it to plants, dilute it 1 part comfrey tea to 10 parts water. Warning: comfrey tea is stinky. Really stinky. So keep a lid on it, and put it somewhere out of the way.

Mulching with a wheelbarrow and shovel

how to mulch

There are two times of year best suited for spreading mulch. Spread in autumn to give your bed an extra layer of insulation over winter and to stop any seeds from germinating during warm spells. Or spread in spring after losing mulch during the worst winter weather.

1. Clear away any leaves, debris and sticks from your beds.

2. Water if your beds are dry from no recent rainfall. Mulch can help seal in moisture.

3. Weed before you mulch; one of the main advantages of mulching is that it helps to prevent weed growth.

4. Spread mulch using a shovel from your wheelbarrow or shake mulch from your bag into small piles. Then use a rake to spread the mulch, being gentle as you get close to the base of any perennial plants and shrubs. Spread the mulch about 2.5–5 cm (2–4 in) thick. If the mulch is spread too thin, then weeds can push through. If the mulch is spread too thick, it prevents water from reaching the soil.

where to grow

in the ground

PROS:
- *Usually more economical than other methods as there's no requirement for additional building materials or expensive pots*
- *You can get started with growing relatively quickly*
- *It's the best way of accessing the soil's natural ecosystem and water table*

CONS:
- *If you live in a colder climate, the soil may remain cold for longer in the spring, which can delay plant growth*
- *Planting and maintaining often require a bent back*

preparing beds in the ground

First, mark out new beds with stakes and string – and if there are pathways between beds, mark them out also. If there's grass, make sure it's cut short and lay cardboard over the whole site to act as an extra light barrier to stop the grass growing.

Water the cardboard a little until it's damp, before mulching on a thick (10–12.5-cm/4–5-in) layer of compost where the beds are situated. You can use a mix of organic matter and compost to create the bed. Layer the least decomposed at the bottom, leaving the finest tilth at the top. You can plant into the beds straight away.

If the site is particularly clogged with brambles or woodier weeds (bindweed and docks, I'm looking at you), grapple with removing them properly by digging out with a sharp trowel before creating a new growing patch there. If, accidentally, a tiny bit of root remains, keep removing any shoots as soon as they appear until the plant's root system is exhausted enough to give up.

I top up the compost by about 2.5 cm (1 in) each winter, and I find that if I use really great, mostly homemade compost, this is sufficient to get two to three healthy crops each year out of the same plot. It's worth experimenting and keeping notes to see what works best for you and your soil.

Create whatever shape of bed you like, although it's good to keep in mind that straight lines with uniform widths and lengths work out as most time-efficient by far for preparing, planting, weeding and harvesting.

paths

For paths, I have a mixture of grass and wood chips. The grass looks lovely but takes more maintenance because it has to be edged and mown about twice a month to stop it from encroaching into the growing space, and sometimes more regularly than that if the weather has been warm and wet.

For wood chip paths, I place cardboard on the grass and scatter the wood chip on top until I can no longer see the cardboard – I use a 7.5-cm (3-in) layer of wood chip.

I make my own wood chip here, but some tree surgeons will drop free wood

chips at allotment sites which can be an inexpensive way to create pathways in a cutting patch. A thin layer of soil or compost is equally fine. By the time everything has grown in the beds you won't even see the paths, and they require little to no maintenance for the whole growing season.

NOTE

If using wood chips, make sure the wood chips do not spill into the beds. Keep them as neatly as you can on the paths only. As they decompose they can alter the pH of the soil and alter the levels of nutrients too.

in raised beds

PROS:

- *They can be used in areas that have very poor soil, contaminated soil or no soil at all*
- *It can be a great way to help make an extra few layers of drainage if your ground soil has a tendency to be waterlogged*
- *Filling the raised bed with compost reduces weeds*
- *Containing the soil can prevent water run-off*
- *It can eliminate bending or stretching to ground level and makes routine garden work easier on the back and knees*
- *They warm quicker than the ground in spring, good for slightly early plantings*
- *Bottoms can be screened with mesh to keep out burrowing pests*
- *The sides help deter pets and children from walking over your plants*

CONS:

- *Building raised beds requires start-up work and investment*
- *Raised beds mean that you must buy in huge amounts of compost or make a lot of your own to fill the beds*
- *It's difficult to remove and replenish the depleted compost*
- *It can be difficult to get equipment inside raised beds, which can make it more difficult to hoe, weed and harvest*
- *Raised beds get warmer, sometimes too warm for roots, in very hot weather*
- *They get colder during cold snaps, so over-wintering plants can be harder*
- *Require more watering as they dry out quicker*

preparing raised beds

A raised bed can be a freestanding box or frame, usually with no bottom, simply holding an additional 15–30 cm (6–12 in) of compost or topsoil above ground level. It can also refer to raised mounds of soil with stones or blocks keeping the soil in place. Sometimes there is no frame at all and the compost is simply mounded up.

Choose the material you would like to edge your raised bed. Place stones or rocks in position.

If using wood, avoid painted or treated wood – it may leach chemicals into the soil. Secure the sides together. The taller the sides, the more pressure they will be under from the soil – add cross-supports to frames taller than 30 cm (12 in).

If placing on a grassed area, make sure the grass is cut short and lay cardboard over the whole site as an extra light barrier to stop the grass growing.

Water the cardboard a little until it's damp, before filling the raised frame with compost.

Plant straight into the beds.

in containers

PROS:

- *Ideal for courtyard gardens that don't have open ground to grow in*
- *Ideal when growing space is limited, for example on balconies, windowsills and by front doors*
- *Containers give you a lot of control over growing conditions, as you can tailor the pH and your care to whatever you're growing*
- *You can move containers in and out of sun or indoors in winter*
- *Containers are also a good way to avoid soil-borne diseases and insect pests*

CONS:

- *Containers do take more plant care since the soil dries out quickly*
- *There will be a finite amount of resources in the container, so choose the biggest pot possible to hold more supply – this can be expensive. (Large containers also dry out less quickly)*
- *You'll need to research the watering and fertilizing needs of the plants you grow as they'll be less self-sufficient than in the ground*

- *For best results, you'll need to replace the potting compost annually, and regular feeding is required to replenish nutrients for the plants as they grow*
- *Insufficient drainage and over-watering can both cause seedlings, cuttings and plants to rot*

preparing containers

Anything that can hold soil and plants can become a container.

Holes in the bottom are essential to make sure there's sufficient drainage. If there aren't holes, use a drill to make enough.

Cover the hole with a crock – a crock is a broken piece of ceramic or rock that won't sit flush against your drainage hole. Its purpose is to stop soil getting clogged in the drainage hole, and from falling out of the bottom; it only lets the water drain through.

You can add a layer of gravel or horticultural grit to improve drainage even more and avoid any soil getting waterlogged. If the bottom of the container is flat place the container up on feet or stones, or place it on gravel which will allow the water to drain out properly.

Add the best compost you can get your hands on. Multi-purpose does best.

If growing an ericaceous plant – be sure to choose acidic ericaceous compost.

seed essentials

Seeds, clockwise from bottom left: nasturtium, calendula, Amaranthus, orach, scabious, nigella, sweet pea

what is a seed?

A seed is a mature ovule with an embryo (tiny, under-developed plant) and food reserves protected by a seed coat.

A seed contains everything it needs to begin a life as a little plant. All that is required to wake the seed from dormancy are the correct conditions for that particular seed (light and temperature) and consistent moisture to break the seed coat.

what seeds to choose?

First and foremost you should make your shortlist full of the plants that you love; be it for their colour, scent, flowers, texture or foliage.

The next step is to figure out which of those shortlisted plants will thrive in your growing conditions. The seed packet should help you out with information on whether to grow in sun, part-shade or full shade.

Cosmos seedling

understanding seed packets

The seed packet is a miniature biography of the plant.

ON THE FRONT

- *Most packets will show a picture or illustration of what you can expect the plant to look like at maturity*

ON THE BACK

- *There will be a brief description of the plant*
- *There will be short and distilled sowing information containing the following:*
  - *What season it is best to sow*
  - *Whether it's preferable to sow it direct into the ground or into seed cell modules under cover to then transfer after frosts*
  - *Whether it has any special requirements to aid germination*
- *Look out for other useful information about that plant, sometimes written but may sometimes be given as an illustration or numbers*

PLANT TYPE

This will determine whether it is an annual, biennial or perennial (see plant glossary on page 28).

ASPECT

This tells you whether it needs to be grown in full sun, or can handle part shade or requires shade.

SPACING

This tells you how close together to plant your seedlings.

DAYS TO MATURITY

This is an approximation of how long a plant takes to develop and reach maturity. It can change depending on your climate and light levels, and whether you started the seed in autumn or spring.

HEIGHT

This tells you how tall the plant will likely get by maturity. Check this bit to see if it is a climber and will therefore need extra support and something to climb.

plant glossary

annuals

Plants that germinate, grow, flower and set seed all in one growing season.

half-hardy annual

Annuals that require warmth to develop and won't tolerate winter wet and cold. They are at risk of not surviving a frost but can be sown under cover before the last frost date.

EXAMPLES: *Cobaea*, cosmos, nasturtium, *Nicotiana*, snapdragon, stock, sweet pea

tender annual

Heat-loving, cold-shy annuals. They need both warmth in the air and warmth in the ground to germinate and to put on any good growth.

EXAMPLES: *Celosia*, marigold, zinnia

hardy annual

Annuals that can tolerate cold weather. These are generally happier in the ground than in containers. They can be planted out before winter to flower in early summer. The longer they have to adjust to the increasingly cold weather the hardier they'll be. Or sow them in modules in autumn and over-winter them under cover. They can be sown again in early spring for later summer flowers.

EXAMPLES: *Ammi*, bells of Ireland, calendula, cornflower, *Cerinthe*, *Daucus carota*, larkspur, nigella

Clockwise from top left: nasturtium 'Milkmaid'; Ammi magus; cosmos 'Rubenza'; sweet pea 'Leominster Boy'

Clockwise from top left: sweet rocket; rose 'Roald Dahl', Hydrangea paniculata 'Limelight'; foxglove and rose 'Litchfield Angel'

biennial

Plants that germinate and grow leaves in their first year, and after a period of cold (this is called vernalization or cold stratification), they flower and set seed in their second year. Usually sown in early summer to flower the following late spring or early summer

EXAMPLES: angelica, dianthus, foxglove, *Hesperis*, hollyhock, Icelandic poppy, *Lunaria*, wallflower

perennials

Perennials are plants that are expected to live for more than two years.

short-lived perennial

Most perennials will live for many, many years, but there are a few that don't have such a long lifespan and will only live for three, four or five years.

EXAMPLES: *Aquilegia, Verbena bonariensis*

herbaceous perennial

Perennials that have non-woody stems that die back down to the ground each year, before sending fresh shoots up again in spring.

EXAMPLES: *Achillea, Alchemilla mollis, Aruncus,* aster, astilbe, *Astrantia, Campanula, Cirsium,* coreopsis, delphinium, *Dicentra, Eryngium, Eupatorium,* gaura, *Geum,* hellebore, *Leucanthemum,* lupin, *Monarda, Nepeta,* nerine, oregano, peony, *Perovskia, Persicaria, Phlomis,* phlox, *Polemonium, Primula,* salvia, *Sanguisorba,* scabious, sedum, *Silene, Tellima, Thalictrum, Veronica*

perennials treated as annuals

Plants that will flower from seed in one growing season and, depending on local climate, will be perennial. They can be over-wintered in their native climates, bulking out and performing better in the subsequent years.

EXAMPLES: *Amaranthus, Echinacea, Rudbeckia*

understanding the importance of light

Plants measure the length of night. Some plants are long-day plants and others short-day plants and so flower accordingly. It's important to note that these sensitivities to light-length cues are relative to the specific plants and can vary. Some long-day plants may have different critical threshold hours of darkness periods, and the same applies to short-day plants.

long-day plants

Long-day plants typically require a day length exceeding a critical threshold, such as 12–14 hours of daylight, to trigger flowering. This means they will automatically flower once the minimum number of daylight hours arrives, no matter how far along they are in growth. To avoid plants being small when the flowering is triggered, it's best to sow earlier in the season to give them more time to grow.

LONG-DAY PLANT EXAMPLES:

Ammi, aster, calendula, cornflowers, dill, lavatera, larkspur, nigella, *Phacelia*, poppy, *Rudbeckia*, strawflower, sweet pea, sweet William, snapdragon, statice, sunflower

Clockwise from top left: cosmos 'Apricotta' and Panicum miliaceum *'Violaceum'; Amaranthus 'Velvet Curtains';* Nicotiana *self seeded garden mix; zinnia 'Zinderella Lilac'*

short-day plants

Short-day plants typically require a day length shorter than 12 hours of daylight. Some short-day plants benefit from being exposed to short-day lengths as seedlings because this may encourage them to flower before the 12 hours of daylight threshold is reached when they're mature.

SHORT-DAY PLANT EXAMPLES:

chrysanthemum, cosmos, dahlia, *Gomphrena*, zinnia

day-neutral plants

Some plants are not affected by the day length to flower, they just need a requisite amount of time and favourable conditions to reach full maturity – these are called day-neutral plants.

DAY-NEUTRAL PLANT EXAMPLES:

Amaranthus, *Cobaea*, *Nicotiana*, phlox, stocks, *Tagetes*, *Verbascum*, viola

applying this to sowing

All this means that some seeds are better to start in autumn, so they have the chance to get as big as possible before the daylight length triggers their flowering. For example, *Ammi* (a long-day plant) sown in autumn will reach heights of 2.13–2.44 m (7–8 ft) before the flowers are triggered to open. Compare this to spring-sown *Ammi*, which will only reach between 0.91–1.5 m (3–5 ft) before the day length triggers flowering.

- *Hardiness levels can impact over-wintering abilities, so some long-day plants are still sometimes better sown in spring. Sunflowers, for example, are not tolerant of frost and are a quick-growing crop, so do best from spring sowing*
- *Short-day plants are triggered to flower when the day length is shorter*
- *Many plants stop active growth when the day length is very short in winter, so it's unwise to sow seeds in the middle of the winter season*
- *All seedlings need plenty of sunlight to thrive (see Troubleshooting: thin tall stems on page 107)*

understanding the importance of temperature

The breaking of seed dormancy is often triggered by exposure to a period of cold (cold stratification) or heat (warm stratification).

- *Many seeds germinate best with the soil temperature in a range of 18–24°C (64–75°F). The desired temperature range varies depending on the seed type*

- *When sowing seeds that require a period of cold, it is recommended to sow them in the autumn, around six to eight weeks before the first frost. That way they'll naturally be exposed to winter's cold temperatures. If sowing in the spring instead, pop the seeds in an air-tight container in the fridge or freezer for a week or two before sowing to mimic the cold conditions they need*

- *For seeds that require warmth, sow when the soil is still warm, or warms again in spring, or use heat mats beneath your seed trays to speed up the germination process*

- *If using heat mats, it's best to take the trays off the heat mats once germination has occurred. Heat mats can coddle the plants too much, encourage weaker root growth and can dry out your seed trays very quickly. Tender plants exposed to too much heat over winter can suffer badly from cold shock once planted out*

seed
tool kit

seed tool kit

Pots, seed trays and cell trays

Multi-purpose peat-free potting compost and/or home-made compost

Plant name tags and permanent marker pen

Trowel

Horticultural fleece

Organic comfrey or seaweed fertilizer

Watering can

Dibber

Hori hori (weeding and planting knife)

Secateurs/garden snips

OPTIONAL TOOL KIT EXTRAS

Horticultural grit

Propagator lids

Heat mat

Grow light

Vermiculite, perlite and coir

Soil tamp

Seedling pricker

Spade and/or shovel

Hoe

Garden gloves

Rake

Garden fork

Twine

Stakes

Wheelbarrow

Spacer stick (a stick marked with your most commonly used spacings)

Cardboard

Widger or butter knife, to slide seedlings out of cells and trays once ready to plant out

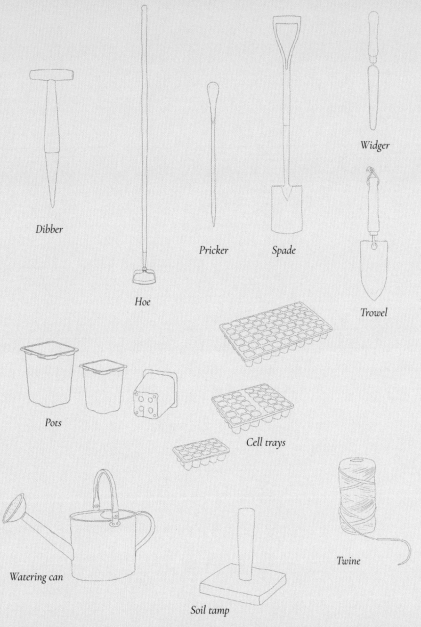

Dibber

Hoe

Pricker

Spade

Widger

Trowel

Pots

Cell trays

Watering can

Soil tamp

Twine

pots and
other vessels

Anything that can hold soil and provide drainage can be used to start seeds in – from eggshells to augmented plastic food storage boxes. But if you want to invest in a long-lasting kit that is designed for seedlings, then here is what I recommend.

my favourite trays and pot sizes

- *Go for sturdy cell trays – they shouldn't make a rustling noise when picked up. The best ones are completely rigid*
- *For the home gardener, smaller cell trays are preferable. You can always cut cell trays in half or thirds if you want to sow fewer of each type of plant – seeds have specific germination requirements and growing speeds, so it's better to sow different plant types separately*
- *Find some propagator lids that fit your cell tray size. The lids are especially helpful for using in tandem with a heat mat. Also helpful for when you want to retain a humid environment for surface-sown seeds*
- *Having the option of a propagator tray to sow tiny seeds is useful; you can then prick out seedlings into cell trays*
- *Some seedlings are bigger, grow quickly, or have long tap roots – sowing straight into pots can be helpful*
- *I like potting cell tray plugs into two sizes of pots, depending on the size of the seedling*

SMALL PROPAGATOR TRAYS

17 cm (6¾ in) long/23 cm (9 in) long

CELL TRAYS

Cells 4 cm (1½ in) wide, 4–6 cm (1½–2⅜ in) deep

POTS (SQUARE SHAPED)

7 cm (2¾ in)/ 9 cm (3½ in) wide

seed compost

You want your seed compost or 'substrate' (often it is a growing medium containing no actual soil or compost, so can be referred to as a substrate) to be light and fluffy and with plenty of air. You want it to take in water but not to hold on to it excessively.

I have trialled so many 'seed composts'. I find that many off-the-rack bags of seed or potting compost dry out quickly or are too heavy. I have settled on one that does a good job for everything I grow. The medium I have settled on has a mix of coir fibre, organic green waste compost and perlite.

A safe bet is to choose a bag of peat-free multi-purpose compost and mix perlite or horticultural grit into it to add extra drainage and air. It's worth experimenting to see what sort of mix works best for your conditions.

THE EASY SEED COMPOST RECIPE

6 parts 'multi-purpose' compost

1 part perlite/grit

Mix well.

THE ULTIMATE SEED COMPOST RECIPE

3 parts coir fibre : 3 parts sifted compost

½ part perlite

½ part vermiculite

Mix well.

how to prepare
a seed tray

Fill seed trays with your seed compost mix. Bang the seed tray on the table to ensure any air bubbles in the compost collapse, or gently press your fingers into the cells (be careful not to over-compact the soil here – air and oxygen is essential for germination).

1. Fill cells where the compost has collapsed from an air bubble.

2. Scrape over the top of the tray with your hand or tamping tool to remove excess compost to avoid over-filling trays, and to avoid losing seeds when watering.

3. Even distribution and compaction of the potting compost will help with the consistent watering of individual cells.

4. For larger seeds, dib (pushing a dent in the soil with a dibber) a little hole to place them in.

5. For smaller seeds, simply sow them onto the surface of the compost.

6. Try to put just one or two seeds maximum in each cell to minimize the need for pricking out.

7. Planting seeds too deep is one of the major causes of low seed germination.

8. Make sure the seed is making contact with the compost surface – if necessary press the seed gently onto it with your finger or a tamp; this is known as tamping.

9. Check if seeds need light (surface sow) or darkness (cover lightly with compost) to germinate.

10. If darkness is required, lightly cover the seed with compost no more than twice as deep as the size of the seed. Alternatively, if seeds need darkness you can also cover your seed tray with an upturned, empty gravel tray to create a dark space.

11. Sit the sown seed tray in a tray of water until the surface has darkened with moisture.

12. Watering from below ensures the seeds won't be washed away and that all the compost in the cell is moist, not just the very top layer.

vermiculite or propagator lids for retaining moisture

Many seeds require light for germination – this means they need to be surface sown to ensure that the seed is still exposed to consistent moisture in order to break the seed coat.

You can use a light top layer or vermiculite on which to sow the seed. Vermiculite takes in and holds onto water, ensuring the surface doesn't dry out as quickly. Sprinkled lightly on the surface of seed trays once the seeds have been sown, it acts like a light mulch and can help retain moisture in the soil allowing for less regular watering. For particularly small, surface-sown seeds that can easily be planted too deep, sprinkle the vermiculite first, then sow the seed.

Alternatively, it is worth placing a clear propagator lid over the seed pots or trays for surface-sown seeds. It will create a humid environment, trapping the escaping moisture and returning it to the soil surface.

Propagator lids are also great for creating a micro-environment that is a little warmer than the external air temperatures, which can speed up germination.

Remove propagator lids once germination has occurred for the seedling to access oxygen. But you can replace them at night to protect more tender seedlings against cold snaps.

how to direct sow

Whether they dislike root disturbance, or they require fluctuating temperatures to initiate germination, some seeds thrive from being sown directly into prepared earth.

1. Rake the bed, ensuring there are no big lumps on the surface – it is often described as a 'fine tilth'.

2. Mark where you would like your rows – it is helpful if you lay down a stake or a cane for straightness.

3. Using a stick or cane, make a shallow rill along the row.

4. Sow your seeds thinly.

5. If light is required for germination, leave uncovered.

6. If darkness is required, gently sprinkle compost over the top of your rows.

7. Leave a little stake at the end of each row to remind you where your seedlings will come up.

8. Water in.

9. Water when the weather is dry; this is especially required to keep the soil moist before germination occurs.

10. You can cover the bed with mesh or horticultural fleece if birds eating the seeds become a problem.

cotyledons vs.
true leaves

The first thing you will see sprouting
up from the soil are the cotyledons.
Cotyledons provide the baby seedling
with nourishment until the true leaves
rise above them and they can start to
photosynthesize and make their own food.

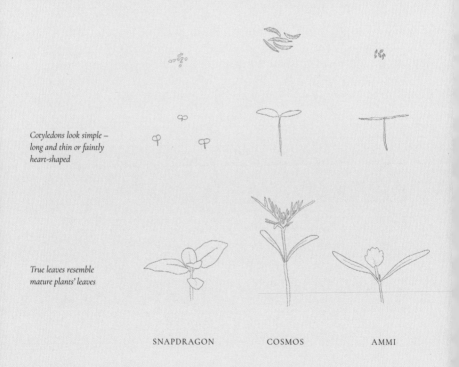

*Cotyledons look simple –
long and thin or faintly
heart-shaped*

*True leaves resemble
mature plants' leaves*

SNAPDRAGON   COSMOS   AMMI

when and how
to water

If you water from above, it's hard to tell when the whole cell has been watered and you run the risk of only watering the very top layer of the compost, which can cause a number of issues. It can cause the bottom half to dry out completely and form a crust between the wet soil and dry soil. This can lead to poor drainage in the cell and it will eventually prohibit the growth of your seedlings' roots. If you do have to water from above, try turning the rose pointing skywards so the water goes up with velocity but falls much more gently onto the seed trays.

The ideal way of watering your seedlings is from underneath.

1. *Fill a gravel tray with water. If you don't have a gravel tray, any vessel that can hold water and is bigger than the seed tray will do.*
2. *Place your seed trays in the water bath for an hour or so, or until the surface of your seed tray turns darker with moisture.*
3. *Remove your seed trays.*

To avoid overwatering, a good rule is to wait to water seedlings when the surface of the tray begins to dry out. When you're still waiting for germination you want to keep the surface moist. Another tip is to lift your tray and weigh it, get a sense of how heavy it is after watering and how light it gets when it's dry. If it feels light, give it good water. If it feels heavy still, leave it for a little longer before watering again.

good circulation practices

When I started growing with Paris Alma, my business partner, my seedlings started getting much healthier. Perhaps two sets of hands are better at tending than just one, but I put it down to how much emphasis Paris puts on good circulation for the seedlings. She insists that there are just a handful of weeks in the whole year where the doors and windows should be shut. Only when the hardest cold never lifts in the day do the hatches remain closed; otherwise, she throws open the doors and opens the windows. As soon as the spring starts to warm, she goes a step further and the trays of seedlings come out every morning to bask, returning to the comfort of the greenhouse before the evening settles in. The only exception being tender or cold intolerant seedlings like zinnias – they get coddled under cover for a little while longer. The result of these practices is far fewer pests and less disease, and happier, healthier little plants.

1. *Sow thinly to avoid seedlings with no space between them.*

2. *Sow or prick out and pot on to individual cells.*

3. *Open windows and doors of your greenhouse or polytunnel during the day when the temperatures are at least above 5°C (41°F) to get good airflow.*

4. *Let your seed trays have an outdoor 'holiday' by bringing them outside on warm and sunny days and bringing them inside again overnight.*

sowing guides

Amaranthus

Amaranthus *looks incredible in the garden, the perfect late-summer and autumnal filler, providing texture, structure and colour. They are easy to grow – and in fact, in warmer climates, they can be so prolific that they can become invasive.*

PLANT TYPE: Half-hardy annual
ASPECT: Full sun
SPACING: 30 cm (12 in) apart
DAYS TO MATURITY: 65–75 approx
HEIGHT: 0.91–1.22 m (3–4 ft)

Best sown direct after the last frost has passed and the soil has warmed. They benefit from a little light, so surface sow and barely cover with compost. Use a propagator lid to help keep the soil surface moist. They benefit from warmth, so use a heat mat to speed up germination. Germination occurs fairly easily and quickly. When you see it begin, remove the lid – but replace it for extra protection on cooler nights. Can also be sown under cover in a frost-free greenhouse in spring. I like to sow in trays and prick out to grow into individual cells when large enough to handle. If there's a late frost, bring seedlings indoors to make sure they survive and put them back in the greenhouse the following morning. Plant out after the last frost. If it's a mild winter, seeds dropped by last year's plants will gently self-sow and germinate when the weather warms the soil.

Keep potting on if there's still cold weather occurring. Avoid letting them get stressed. If they send out flowers too early, which can happen when they're stressed, they won't have the power to reach their full growing potential. Benefits from pinching to encourage more side shoots. Pinch when seedling is 20 cm (8 in) and 30 cm (12 in), or when it has at least 3–5 sets of true leaves, to promote side branches to make it much easier to use in arrangements. The root systems are fairly shallow so you can plant over narcissi or tulips to maximize growing space.

Harvest when the seed heads have about three-quarters of their little florets open.

TIPS

Leave un-pinched for grand, architectural stems.

Amaranths are ready for seed harvesting when they're not fully dried and when you rub the flowers with your hands, lots of seeds are released. Strip the flowers into a bucket and sieve the seeds out.

Cosmos

Very easy to grow from seed, cosmos will give you many, many flowers – the more you cut the more they give. With lovely fronds on foliage, delicate swaying stems and pretty flowers that come in a range of colours, cosmos are a staple of the summer cutting garden.

PLANT TYPE: Half-hardy annual
ASPECT: Full sun
SPACING: 30 cm (12 in) apart
DAYS TO MATURITY: 75–90 approx
HEIGHT: 0.91–1.22 m (3–4 ft)

Sow under cover in spring, and plant out after the last frost— or direct sow when the weather and soil have warmed after the frosts have passed.

Seeds are large, easy to handle, and germinate quickly and readily.

Cosmos are sensitive to light levels and are triggered into flowering when the days are slightly shorter. If you sow them too early in spring, the flowering will be triggered when they are still tiny seedlings. To have the biggest, most productive plants that will give you the most flowers, you want as much of the growth to happen during the longer days, but also have had them exposed to shorter days so you don't have to wait until the end of the summer for flowering to be triggered. For this to happen, start the seeds under cover earlier in spring, around the time of the spring equinox.

Pinch out the top of the seedling when it is 20–30 cm (8–12 in) tall to encourage bushier growth and more flowers.

TIP

Very easy to grow from seed, and they will give you many, many flowers – the more you cut the more they give.

Orach

Orach is such a beautiful foliage filler.
I use it in designs to take advantage of its
dramatic and towering plumes of seeds.

PLANT TYPE: Hardy annual
ASPECT: Full sun
SPACING: 30 cm (12 in) apart
DAYS TO MATURITY: 70–80 approx
HEIGHT: 1.2–2.1 m (4–7 ft)

Best sown directly in spring, after the last frost, where they are to grow and flower. Seeds benefit from warmth for germination, so use a heat mat and propagator lid to speed up germination.

Pinch out the top of the seedling when 20 cm (8 in) tall to encourage bushier growth and more flowers. Or leave for ridiculously tall stems – amazing for using in large-scale installations.

Perfect for drying. Harvest just as the seed pods have developed, hang upside down to dry.

TIP

Self-sows everywhere, you'll only need to sow these once to have them forever! Cut them back before the seeds form to avoid them seeding in places you'd rather not have them.

Cerinthe

Beloved by the bees, this is the best early foliage plant for late spring and early summer bouquets. It has lovely nodding snakeheads in silvery-blue with purple flowers, and it readily self-sows – excellent for a time-strapped gardener.

PLANT TYPE: Half-hardy annual
ASPECT: Full sun
SPACING: 23–30.5 cm (9–12 in) apart
DAYS TO MATURITY: 65–70 approx
HEIGHT: 61 cm (2 ft)

Best sown under cover in autumn to get the biggest, most productive plants. Protect from hard frosts and plant out in spring. *Cerinthe* seeds and seedlings are large, so sow them into larger cells or small pots to ensure they have enough room. Or sow under cover in early spring to plant out after the last frost. Cover with compost as darkness aids germination. They germinate quickly and bulk up relatively quickly too. Pot on from seed cells if necessary. Some seeds germinate as two seedlings. Either sacrifice one, or lever the cell from the tray and gently separate the two seedlings, potting them on in separate cells.

Cerinthe collapse in frost but mostly bounce back quickly. Protect with frost-cloths from particularly hard frosts (extended periods below -5°C/23°F)

TIP

Place freshly cut stems into boiling water for 10 seconds when harvesting to avoid wilting after harvest.

Poppy

With their tissue-like, papery petals, poppies are a beautiful flower to grow. They burst from their casings and bring joy and colour to the garden through spring and summer. They're perfect for pollinators too.

PLANT TYPE: Hardy annual
ASPECT: Full sun
SPACING: 23 cm (9 in) apart
DAYS TO MATURITY: 60–75 approx
HEIGHT: 61 cm (2 ft)

Annual poppies do not like their roots being disturbed, so it's best to direct sow in spring. Benefits from light to germinate, so surface sow or very lightly cover with compost. You can start them under cover in autumn; just be extra gentle when transplanting. Wait until the roots have filled up the cell before potting on to help minimize the disturbance of the roots.

Netting support is helpful to keep the plants upright no matter what the weather.

Harvest when the buds are just cracking open and sear stems in boiling water or with a flame as soon as you harvest for the best vase life.

TIP

They benefit from the cold stratification of winter, so pre-chill seeds if starting them under cover. Let them grow on in cooler temperatures.

Phlox

Phlox have such unassuming sweetness and make the perfect sidekick flower to focal flowers. The annual varieties come in a range of creams, mauves, pinks and blues. Great in pots!

PLANT TYPE: Half-hardy annual
ASPECT: Full sun
SPACING: 23 cm (9 in) apart
DAYS TO MATURITY: 60–65 approx
HEIGHT: 30.5–61 cm (1–2 ft)

Phlox are slow growing, so sow under cover in very early spring and plant out after the last frost. Seeds require darkness to germinate, so cover or place in a dark space until you spot germination. Check under the cover daily and remove the cover when germination has begun. Cover any seeds not yet germinated with a little extra compost to ensure darkness.

Make sure to plant in a spot that drains well. I find they do best in warm summers. Requires netting support to get straight stems.

TIP

Keep pinching out the flowers as they start to appear, to encourage longer, more workable stems.

Bells of Ireland

Mesmerizing spires that make a perfect foliage flower. Outstanding summer and autumn filler for filling big jugs or filling out summer bouquets. Especially lovely when they have gentle, architectural curves to them.

PLANT TYPE: Half-hardy annual
ASPECT: Full sun
SPACING: 23 cm (9 in) apart
DAYS TO MATURITY: 90–110 approx
HEIGHT: 61–91.5 cm (2–3 ft)

These flowers benefit from a period of cold stratification before germination – pop them in the freezer a week before sowing. Once chilled, place in water to soak for 24 hours. They need light for germination, so leave seeds uncovered and use a propagator lid to keep the soil moist. Sow under cover in modules in spring and plant out after the last frost. Or sow them direct in early spring, before the frosts have passed but when the soil has warmed a little. The freeze/thaw activity will help break their seed coat. This allows them to be exposed to fluctuating temperatures that will aid their germination. Water the area you'll be sowing well before placing seeds. Make a line in the ground and sprinkle them in at around 23 cm (9 in) apart. Barely cover with soil.

The stems can develop little spines as the flower matures, so be careful when harvesting.

TIPS

If germination is slow, agitate the surface of the compost a little with your finger! These prefer a cooler climate, so they'll slow down in growth as the season heats up. The leaves sometimes cause skin reactions – you can remove them before working with them.

Cobaea

These sweet nodding bells come in a delicate cream or soft purple and open on winding vines that can grow 3–6 m (10–20 ft) in one season! It covers our arches all summer and into autumn, and we cut plenty of the flowers and tendrils for bud vases and bridal bouquets.

PLANT TYPE: Half-hardy annual
ASPECT: Full sun
SPACING: 15–30.5 cm (6–12 in) apart
DAYS TO MATURITY: 120 approx
HEIGHT: 3–6 m (10–20 ft)

Cobaea need a long time to reach maturity. Sow under cover early in the year in late winter. You'll need to protect the seeds from frosts and keep the seedlings warm if sowing this early. Warmth for germination will help speed up the process too. Sowing the seed on its edge can help to avoid rot. Be careful not to plant the seed too deep.

Plant out seedlings after the last frost. Pot on into larger pots if the frosts stop you from planting out. Make sure you have a strong trellis for the vines to climb. Tie in the first 50 cm (20 in) of growth to encourage the vine upwards.

TIP

Cobaea needs a long growing period before they flower. Start in the greenhouse or bright windowsill early, in January or February.

Calendula

An easy to grow cut-flower, the more you cut calendula the more they give. The petals are edible and brighten up any salad. Can also be turned into a salve for tired skin. A quick and easy seed to germinate – a great beginner plant.

PLANT TYPE: Hardy annual
ASPECT: Full sun
SPACING: 23–30 cm (9–12 in) apart
DAYS TO MATURITY: 60–75 approx
HEIGHT: 61 cm (2 ft)

Best sown under cover in autumn to get the biggest, most productive plants. Protect from hard frosts and plant out in spring.

Calendula have large seeds that tend to push their way up to the surface. Dib a little hole in each cell, twice the depth of the seed, then place a seed in each and cover them with compost. They benefit from a little warmth, around 21°C (70°F). If warmth from a heat mat is given, you'll likely see germination within a week.

Direct sow in early spring to flower in later summer. Or sow in modules and plant out. They prefer their initial growing period to be in cooler weather. Heat will slow them down. So don't leave it too late in the spring to sow them.

Benefits from pinching to encourage more side shoots. Pinch when seedling is 20 cm (8 in) and 30 cm (12 in). Or when it has at least 3–5 sets of true leaves.

TIPS

Harvest when the flowers are just opening. Once the flowers have been pollinated, the petals will quickly curl and wilt.
Cut seed heads from your plants, calendula is an aggressive self-seeder!

Corncockle

Slender, waving stems with the most elegant, reflexed petals that have delicate freckles – this is one of the most chic things to have in your garden, not to mention your flower arrangements.

PLANT TYPE: Half-hardy annual
ASPECT: Full sun
SPACING: 15–23 cm (6–9 in) apart
DAYS TO MATURITY: 90–100 approx
HEIGHT: 61–91.5 cm (2–3 ft)

A quick and easy crop to grow. Seeds require light for germination so surface sew or barely cover with compost. Best sown under cover in autumn to get the biggest, most productive plants. Protect from hard frosts and plant out in spring. Or sow from late winter through spring for shorter, more delicate flowers the same year. Can also be sown in modules. Such a quick crop that you can do multiple sowings for a successional supply.

Once planted out in the ground, the floppy fresh growth of the tips benefits from netting support to get the straightest stems.

Harvest when buds are halfway open to achieve the best vase life.

NOTE
Toxic to chickens and sheep.

Dill

The perfect summery filler for everything – bouquets, arrangements, clouds of it in vases on its own. It looks spectacular in the garden too, with its starry yellow flowers.

PLANT TYPE: Half-hardy annual
ASPECT: Full sun
SPACING: 30 cm (12 in) apart
DAYS TO MATURITY: 90–100 approx
HEIGHT: 0.91–1.22 m (3–4 ft)

For best results sow directly into the ground in autumn for flowers early the following summer. Autumn-sown plants also grow a lot bigger. They benefit from light to germinate, so surface sow or lightly cover with compost. You can also direct sow in spring once the soil has warmed for flowers the same year – they will just be a little shorter in height. They can be started in pots, but always seem to do better germinating while exposed to the elements. Transplanting from a pot into the ground can stress them out too. However, dill grows a long tap-root, so starting them in pots will allow them the space to send down a strong root. If starting indoors, the seeds benefit from a little warmth for germination, so try using a heat mat and a propagator lid.

TIP

Dill is prone to wilting, so it's vital to harvest in the coolest parts of the day and place in water immediately to drink for a few hours somewhere cool before using.

Gomphrena

One of the very best flowers for drying!
These are the sweetest pom-poms of joy,
both fresh and dried.

PLANT TYPE: Half-hardy annual
ASPECT: Full sun
SPACING: 23 cm (9 in) apart
DAYS TO MATURITY: 85–100 approx
HEIGHT: 61 cm (2 ft)

Sow under cover in spring and plant out after the last frost. Start around 8 weeks before the last frost as the young seedlings take a while to mature enough to be planted out. The seeds don't seem to mind darkness or light to germinate, so cover the seeds with a light layer of compost or surface sow. Make sure the surface of the soil does not dry out before germination. *Gomphrena* require warmth for germination so place on a heat mat or sunny windowsill. Move off the heat once germination appears and place in full light.

Best cut for drying when all flowers are open.

TIP

Gomphrena are very easy to grow and are productive – harvest, and more will grow and ripen. However, they are particularly slow to grow and mature; patience is required. They do best in warm summers.

Larkspur

Larkspur is a star of the late spring, early summer cutting garden, with a profusion of airy, tall stems, covered in lovely papery blooms.

PLANT TYPE: Hardy annual
ASPECT: Full sun
SPACING: 23 cm (9 in) apart
DAYS TO MATURITY: 110–120 approx
HEIGHT: 0.91–1.22 m (3–4 ft)

Best sown directly in autumn. The tap root on a larkspur seedling is long and delicate and prefers to be undisturbed. The cooler winter temperatures will also be ideal for germination and for supplying the cool growing period it requires. They particularly like the fluctuating temperatures between day and night. An unheated greenhouse, or outdoors, are the conditions they like best. The only downside to sowing outdoors is that larkspur seeds are prone to rot, so a particularly wet autumn or winter will potentially kill your seeds. Can be sown under cover to avoid this, but because the seeds require cooler temperatures for germination to occur do not place on a heat mat. Cover lightly with compost as the seeds need darkness to germinate. Use a tray to cover if extra darkness is required. Sew a single seed in each cell to avoid having to thin and disturb the roots.

Hardy down to -15°C (5°F), but I have known plants to struggle in very exposed spots in long cold snaps, so protect with horticultural fleece during extreme cold. Keep a close eye on the growth of your undercover-grown seedlings. Pot on as soon as the roots fill the cell and don't let them become rootbound as stress will limit eventual growth.

TIPS

Larkspur need cold stratification to germinate. Pop the seed packet in a freezer for a week before sowing.
The seeds and all parts of this plant are toxic.

Nicotiana

Statuesque flowers that twinkle high above the other plants in the border.

PLANT TYPE: Half-hardy annual
ASPECT: Part shade to full sun
SPACING: 30 cm (12 in) apart
DAYS TO MATURITY: 90–105 approx
HEIGHT: 0.91–1.22 m (3–4 ft)

Sow under cover in late spring. The seeds are tiny! Try your best to sow just one seed per cell. Water from below if sowing in trays. These seeds benefit from a little warmth to germinate so try a heat mat and propagator lid. Remove once germination occurs and plant out when frosts have passed. Alternatively, direct sow when the weather has warmed. *Nicotiana* are light sensitive, so sow when the days are longer at around 14 hours of daylight. Light aids germination, so leave sown on the surface.

TIPS

I find the seedlings prone to damping off, so have good circulation practices, and don't allow the soil to get too cold and damp.
The stems are slightly tacky to the touch when working with them for design work. Avoid using *Nicotiana* in designs with other stems that drop pollen, as the pollen will stick to the *Nicotiana* and it can soon look a mess.

Statice

These are lovely used fresh, I tuck them into arrangements and bouquets to help form a backdrop of colour. They're long-lasting in the vase. They're also the very best flower for drying! They hold their vibrancy, shape and colours really well when dry.

PLANT TYPE: Half-hardy annual
ASPECT: Full sun
SPACING: 30 cm (12 in) apart
DAYS TO MATURITY: 110–120 approx
HEIGHT: 61 cm (2 ft)

Statice is a quick-growing plant and usually has a fast germination too – ideal if your seed trays have some empty cells. Start sowing in early spring. Statice seeds benefit from warmth at around 21°C (70°F) to speed up germination, so pop on a heat mat or use a propagator lid. They need light to germinate so barely cover them with compost, or leave the seeds uncovered and just use a propagator lid to stop the surface from drying out. Make a second and third sowing a few weeks apart to have successional flowers. Statice can be direct sown once the weather and soil have warmed.

The plant forms a rosette of leaves. These can be tinged with red if exposed to cold, but it doesn't do anything to harm or stunt the plant, so don't worry. Harden off before planting out; they require minimal care afterwards. Water well when first planted and for the first week, then water if a dry spell occurs.

Keep cutting stems to encourage more to be sent up to flower for you. To harvest for drying, cut when all flowers are open. Tie up tightly in bunches of 10–15 stems and hang upside down somewhere dry, dark and frost-free.

TIP
Sun exposure to dried flowers can cause colour loss and brittleness.

Malope

Attractive to have in the garden and vase, it will flower for an age and has lovely movement in the stems – a stem of this alone in a bud vase has the power to look abundant yet elegant.

PLANT TYPE: Hardy annual
ASPECT: Full sun
SPACING: 30 cm (12 in) apart
DAYS TO MATURITY: 90–110 approx
HEIGHT: 61–91.5 cm (2–3 ft)

Although a hardy annual, *Malope* dislikes being too cold and damp, so wait until spring and sow under cover. If sowing in autumn, use a heat mat and propagator lid to germinate – remove once germination occurs, but replace a propagator lid or place horticultural fleece over them during cold snaps. Seeds can also be direct sown when the weather and soil have warmed.

Seedlings grow quickly, so pot on if necessary and plant out after the last frost. The mature plants can flop, so support with netting.

For the best vase life, harvest when only a few of the flowers have opened. The other flower buds will continue to open in the vase.

TIP

Malope seeds can benefit from cold stratification to break dormancy, so pop in an airtight container and place them in the fridge for a week or two before sowing.

Cynoglossum

This is such a pretty and quick-growing flower. It's a really useful one to have in the cutting patch – it offers such a dainty and fun bit of colour to designs. It self-seeds so it's useful for the time-strapped gardener.

PLANT TYPE: Half-hardy annual
ASPECT: Full sun
SPACING: 23–30.5 cm (9–12 in) apart
DAYS TO MATURITY: 75–85 approx
HEIGHT: 61–91.5 cm (2–3 ft)

Sow under cover in spring, and plant out after the last frost. Or direct sow when the weather and soil have warmed. Seeds require darkness to germinate, so cover or place in a dark space until you spot germination. These are very quick to grow and flower. Sow every few weeks to have a succession of flowers.

Keep on top of harvesting to prolong flowering; as soon as they run to seed they'll slow down. They love to self-seed, so if you don't want them to, cut all plants back before the seeds begin to drop.

TIP

Cynoglossum are prone to wilting, so it's vital to harvest in the coolest parts of the day and place in water immediately to drink for a few hours somewhere cool before using.

Zinnia

We love the paler zinnias for wedding work and the jazzier colours for late summer meadow designs. There is a parchment-like texture to zinnias, making them robust and long-lasting in the vase.

PLANT TYPE: Half-hardy annual
ASPECT: Full sun
SPACING: 23 cm (9 in) apart
DAYS TO MATURITY: 75–90 approx
HEIGHT: 61–91.5 cm (2–3 ft)

Sow under cover in spring, and plant out after the last frost. Or direct sow when the weather and soil have warmed, if you have a warmer climate. They absolutely do not tolerate a frost or the cold, so protect them from cold nights. Wait to sow until your weather is warmer – or you can sow under cover a little earlier if you need to, because the short day length helps their growth pattern, being short-day plants.

Zinnias prefer not to be transplanted, but as long as you don't let them get rootbound and are gentle when moving them from cells or pots to the ground and water them in well, they will settle absolutely fine either way. Plant them out in full sun (at least 6 hours a day) at a spacing of 23–30 cm (9–12 in). The warmer your climate and your soil, the taller and more vigorous the growth will be. Net them in advance just in case you have a particularly warm summer. They're thirsty plants so require a steady supply of water too. Zinnias are particularly susceptible to powdery mildew. If your summers are humid, then search out mildew-resistant varieties to grow.

Zinnias need to be fully ripe to avoid wilting in the vase. It can be hard to tell if they're ready just by looking at them, so test them with a little shake of the stem. If the flower head wobbles on the top of the stalk, leave it for another day or two. If it remains stiff as you shake, it's ready and ripe. Harvest low into the plant, just above a set of shoots, to encourage the next shoots to be long and strong.

TIPS

These plants are very easy to grow from seed, they thrive in hot summers and the more you pick, the more long, strong stems they will produce.
Change their water regularly as the stems have a habit of building up bacteria quickly.

Nigella

Nigella is also known as Love-In-The-Mist, because of its delicate flowers appearing out from its gauzy fronded foliage. The balloon-like seed pods are just as good as the flowers.

PLANT TYPE: Hardy annual
ASPECT: Full sun
SPACING: 23 cm (9 in) apart
DAYS TO MATURITY: 65–85 approx
HEIGHT: 61 cm (2 ft)

For best results sow directly into well-prepared soil in autumn for flowers early the following summer. Autumn-sewn plants grow a lot bigger. Or sow in modules over winter under cover and plant out in spring. Not as hardy as most hardy annuals, so sow direct under cover in cells if you are prone to cold winters, or if you don't want to run the risk of losing the outdoor ones. You can also direct sow in spring for smaller plants that will flower later in the summer. They have a very delicate root system so go very gently if transplanting from cells to the ground.

Paris always rolls her eyes at me when I try to prick out and save any extra seedlings – they do not do well from pricking out, so she is right to just thin the seedlings. It is not worth the extra effort.

TIP

The seed heads are perfect for drying, as a serious bonus – the seeds can be used in cooking, and the petals are edible too.

Cornflower

Most likely the easiest cutting flower to grow. Classic cornflowers are blue, but there are lovely varieties in pink, blush, cranberry, white, pale blue, purple and many more besides.

PLANT TYPE: Half-hardy annual
ASPECT: Full sun
SPACING: 30 cm (12 in) apart
DAYS TO MATURITY: 65–80 approx
HEIGHT: 0.91–1.22 m (3–4 ft)

Best sown under cover in early autumn to get the biggest, most productive plants. Protect from hard frosts and plant out in spring. Easy to germinate, the seed is quite big, so benefits from being placed in a hole dibbed in the cells and covered with compost. Germination happens quickly and readily. Or direct sow in spring to flower in later summer. Alternatively, if you don't want to direct sow, you can sow in modules in spring and plant out when the seedlings have a strong root system.

Particularly hardy; once germinated, let them grow on in a cooler environment. Make sure they have plenty of light. They grow a big rosette of foliage that not only covers the compost but drinks plenty of water, so ensure to check the soil for its moisture levels regularly. To support its large rosette through winter, cornflower seedlings require a strong root system to have grown before the cold of winter sets in.

TIP

The petals are edible, and also keep their vibrant colour well when dried. Deadhead regularly to keep them flowering and save the petals to brighten up winter cakes, biscuits and salads.

Orlaya

As Orlaya's common name of lace flower suggests, these have the most exquisite lacy petals. An earlier flowering frothy filler, it's ideal for pairing with early summer favourites like sweet peas and roses.

PLANT TYPE: Hardy annual
ASPECT: Full sun
SPACING: 23–30.5 cm (9–12 in) apart
DAYS TO MATURITY: 70–85 approx
HEIGHT: 61–91.5 cm (2–3 ft)

Best sown under cover in autumn to get the biggest, most productive plants, planting out in the late winter or early spring. Alternatively, direct sow in early spring to flower in later summer, but the plants struggle when the temperatures get too warm. The fluctuating temperatures between day and night in autumn and early spring are beneficial. Cover the seed only lightly with compost.

Harvest when the flowers are nearly fully open, otherwise it has a tendency to wilt.

TIP

Orlaya require a period of cold, so try chilling the seed in the fridge two weeks before sowing. Fresh seed is the best for the germination of *Orlaya*. Consider saving your own seed!

Ammi

The perfect filler for the florist – bouquets, or easy arrangements of it in vases on its own. It looks spectacular in the garden, giving a beautiful, long-lasting froth to summer borders. The seed heads are statuesque, which gives interest later in the season.

PLANT TYPE: Half-hardy annual
ASPECT: Full sun
SPACING: 30 cm (12 in) apart
DAYS TO MATURITY: 65–75 approx
HEIGHT: 1.2–1.5 m (4–6 ft)

For best results sow directly into well-prepared soil in autumn for flowers early the following summer. Autumn-sown *Ammi* grows a lot bigger because long daylight hours trigger flowering whatever size it's reached. Or, you can direct sow in spring, when the weather and soil have warmed, for flowers the same year. Alternatively sow under cover in modules and plant out after the last frost. Benefits from a period of cold stratification, so if you're sowing in spring, pop the seeds in an air-tight container and place them in the freezer a week before sowing.

It germinates happily when the days are warm and nights are cool. When the weather warms again in spring, it'll bulk up very quickly given enough space.

Harvest flowers for cutting at dawn or dusk when the plant is at its most hydrated. The stems are ready when the little white flowers are fully open but before the pollen begins to drop.

TIPS

Don't pinch – they are not cut-and-come-again flowers.
They're also great in arrangements once seed heads begin to form. Particularly strong out of water once the seed heads have formed.

Rudbeckia

Rudbeckia *are our go-to late summer crop.* Rudbeckia *varieties have so much variation, from sunny yellows to the most unbelievable sunset shades. It can be overwintered as a perennial if you have mild conditions.*

PLANT TYPE: Short-lived perennial
ASPECT: Full sun
SPACING: 30 cm (12 in) apart
DAYS TO MATURITY: 100–120 approx
HEIGHT: 61 cm (2 ft)

Rudbeckia take a long time to reach maturity, so sow in late winter to very early spring. They need light for germination, so barely cover with compost or use a propagator lid. Seeds prefer warmth to germinate, so use a heat mat and propagator lid to speed up germination. Sensitive to dampness, so don't overwater just keep the soil moist.

Slow to mature into bigger plug plants. Plant out when sizeable in early summer. *Rudbeckia* is a short-lived perennial so will overwinter if we don't have an extreme cold snap.

Harvest when the flower is a couple of days old.

TIP

Can be prone to wilt, so try blanching the stems in boiling water for 10 seconds and let them drink in cool water for a long time before using.

Scabious

Tall, waving stems with the softest pincushion flowers on top, Scabious is one of the most elegant things to have in your garden and in arrangements. They have a great vase life.

PLANT TYPE: Hardy annual
ASPECT: Full sun
SPACING: 30 cm (12 in) apart
DAYS TO MATURITY: 90–100 approx
HEIGHT: 0.91–1.22 m (3–4 ft)

Sow in late winter with a heat mat, when light levels are getting longer, to get the biggest, most productive plants. Scabious have big seeds – dib a hole in each cell before placing a seed in. Light helps germination, so leave uncovered. They can also be direct sown in spring to flower in later summer.

They grow quickly, so they will most definitely require potting on. Protect from hard frosts and plant out in spring. Netting support helps the plants from falling sideways once flowering begins and the stems become top heavy.

TIP

For the longest vase life, harvest when the flower is halfway open.

Panicum

We think this is one of the most elegant, dramatic and gorgeous grasses you can grow, with its swaying black pearls dangling on long tassels! The birds love it, so leave some seed heads for them and you'll have them swooping beautifully through your garden.

PLANT TYPE: Hardy annual
ASPECT: Full sun
SPACING: 30 cm (12 in) apart
DAYS TO MATURITY: 60–100 approx
HEIGHT: 91.5 cm (3 ft)

Best sown directly in spring where they are to grow and flower to get the biggest, most productive plants. They can also be sown in cell trays; just cover lightly with compost.

Plant out after the last frost; needs temperatures of around 18–22°C (64–71°F) to germinate readily.

TIPS

The birds love to eat the ripe seeds; leave some heads standing as natural bird feeders for them into the autumn. *Panicum* will self-sow, and the seeds are easy to harvest yourself, too. *Panicum* are also perfect for drying.

Viola

The loveliest of faces – the viola is so sweet and full of charm. Classic violas are a favourite flower of mine to grow in a window box. They're almost impossible to buy as a cut flower, so growing them is a great way to have something that will make your design work stand out.

PLANT TYPE: Hardy annual
ASPECT: Full sun
SPACING: 15 cm (6 in) apart
DAYS TO MATURITY: 80–90 approx
HEIGHT: 23–30.5 cm (9–12 in)

Start seeds under cover up to 12 weeks before the last frost. Cover lightly with compost as seeds need darkness to germinate. Use a tray to cover if extra darkness is required.

Violas are cold tolerant, so harden off and transplant out when seedlings are big enough, up to two weeks before the last frost date. They can tolerate a light frost, but if the plants are still young protect them from any extreme cold snaps with horticultural fleece. They grow well in pots, or grow them in the ground quite close together for better stem length. I underplant our sweet peas with them. We've found they can handle hot temperatures in the summer in the polytunnel too.

Keep harvesting to encourage more and more flowers.

TIP

I also plant violas in the pot above a layer of narcissus and tulip bulbs, which not only gives a double crop from the smallest space, but when the narcissi and tulips are ready they force the violas to grow upwards for longer, more workable stems. As a bonus, the bulb stems act as support for the more fragile violas.

Strawflower

The best, best, best flower for drying! Papery in nature and they keep their beautiful colours so well.

PLANT TYPE: Half-hardy annual
ASPECT: Full sun
SPACING: 30 cm (12 in) apart
DAYS TO MATURITY: 80–90 approx
HEIGHT: 91.5 cm (3 ft)

Best sown under cover in spring. I find them slow to mature in my cool climate, so I start in early spring to have them flower sooner in the summer to harvest enough before the autumn sets in. They need light to germinate, so barely cover them with compost, or leave them uncovered and use a propagator lid to stop the surface from drying out. Can be direct sown once the weather and soil have warmed.

Plant out after the last frost.

TIP

To dry, harvest on a dry day. Hang upside down out of direct sunlight in a dry, frost-free environment.

Sweet Pea

A fistful of sweet peas – there's nothing better. Some varieties have longer stems, or offer scent or different colours.

PLANT TYPE: Hardy annual
ASPECT: Full sun
SPACING: 20 cm (8 in) apart
DAYS TO MATURITY: 75–90 approx
HEIGHT: 1.5–2.4 m (5–8 ft)

Sow in pots under cover during autumn for the biggest and most productive plants. Overwinter in a sheltered spot with lots of light. Plant out in early spring after careful hardening off. Alternatively, sow under cover from January and then plant out in the later spring.

The young plants can handle a light cold spell, but do protect from hard frosty temperatures with horticultural fleece. If spring-sown, pinch out the growing tips at 15 cm (6 in) tall to encourage bushier growth and more flowers. No need to pinch autumn-sown sweet peas; they will branch naturally. Sweet pea plants enjoy lots of nutrition and cool roots, so water regularly and add a little seaweed fertilizer or comfrey tea.

TIP
Keep harvesting the flowers to encourage more shoots and blooms.

Phacelia

Offering the loveliest lilac froth, Phacelia is one of the easiest things to grow. Not only is it a great filler for bouquets, it will also fill your garden with pollinators. The bees can't get enough of it!

PLANT TYPE: Hardy annual
ASPECT: Full sun
SPACING: 30 cm (12 in) apart
DAYS TO MATURITY: 70–80 approx
HEIGHT: 61–91.5 cm (2–3 ft)

Best sown directly in autumn or spring where they are to grow and flower. A hard winter will wipe out autumn-sown seedlings, but as they're very quick growing save some seed to sow again in spring. Darkness aids germination so cover with a thin layer of compost.

Harvest when the flower head has started to curl around to avoid wilting.

TIP

Self-sows everywhere, you'll only need to sow these once to have them forever! Cut them back before the seeds form to avoid them seeding in places you'd rather not have them.

Snapdragon

There's nothing more striking or glamorous than a bunch of snapdragons. Absolutely stunning en-masse.

PLANT TYPE: Half-hardy annual
ASPECT: Full sun
SPACING: 23 cm (9 in) apart
DAYS TO MATURITY: 100–110 approx
HEIGHT: 61–91.5 cm (2–3 ft)

We sow two plantings: one in autumn and one in spring. Snapdragons are one of the few annuals I sow into a small tray and prick out. The seeds are like dust and I find it hard to sow single seeds into cells. They don't mind being pricked out. Light aids germination, so do not cover the seed with compost. For best germination, place the tray on a heat mat with a propagator lid. Remove the lid once germination occurs and let them grow on away from the heat of the mat. Make sure the seed tray has lots of light.

If you don't want to overwinter, sow under cover from early spring.

Plant out after the last frosts. Netting support is required to keep them upright. Pinching encourages many more blooms.

TIP
Careful – the tiniest seeds!

seedlings

troubleshooting

There are many variables as to why a seedling might have trouble, and it's not always a clear and obvious cause. Here are a number signs to look out for and a suggestion of what might be causing the problem.

yellowing leaves

COLD SHOCK / HUNGRY / OVERWATERING

Check the soil. If it doesn't seem waterlogged, and there hasn't been a cold snap, try placing the tray in a water bath with a little comfrey/seaweed fertilizer mixed in.

To avoid cold shock, make sure you harden your seedlings off slowly to make sure they don't suffer from the change in conditions.

poor root growth / root rot

COMPACTED SOIL / POOR DRAINAGE / OVERWATERING

Try mixing more perlite or horticultural grit into your seed compost to create more air pockets and drainage. Try sitting your seed trays onto trays or gravel for extra drainage from below. Be more gentle when filling your seed trays with compost.

blisters on leaves

OVERWATERING

Overwatering can prevent oxygen and nutrients getting to the roots properly and blisters can appear when the plant is trying to remove excess moisture. Allow your seed compost to almost dry out and water from below, monitoring the tray to remove it from the water bath as soon as the compost turns darker with moisture. Overwatering also gives an increased risk of damping off disease arriving – the pathogens reproduce and infect plants more effectively in wet soils.

curling leaves or leaf abnormalities

EXCESSIVELY LOW OR HIGH HUMIDITY, VIRAL OR FUNGAL INFECTION

Try to keep temperatures stable and encourage good air flow in your growing space. Get rid of any seedlings that are showing signs of fungal or viral infection.

green algae or mould on soil surface

OVERWATERING WHEN COLD

Overwatering when cold, leaving the soil cold and wet, is one of the most common troubleshooting problems. It can cause fungus and lead to damping off disease. Try using a heat mat, and water a little less.

withered stem / leaf drop / collapse

DAMPING OFF – INSUFFICIENT CIRCULATION OR OVERWATERING

Damping off is when a weak seedling succumbs to soil-borne fungi; this usually occurs when the seed is started on soil that's too cold, or overwatering in cold conditions. Insufficient circulation can also encourage fungi to spread. Sow thinly and prick out to individual cells for increased circulation. If damping off disease presents itself, dispose of infected seedlings and compost so it doesn't spread further. Give your seed trays a good wash with hot, soapy water – and even a little spray of bleach can help. Open windows during the day (not during a cold snap) to encourage air flow in your growing space.

no seedling appears

SEED ROT / OVERWATERING / OLD SEED / BADLY STORED SEED / SEED WASHED AWAY FROM OVERHEAD WATERING / SEED EATEN BY PESTS / SEEDS IN NEED OF COLD OR HOT STRATIFICATION / IMPROPER GROWING CONDITIONS PROVIDED / SEEDLING BURIED TOO DEEP

When no seedling appears, it can be a number of problems. The first thing to check is the germination of your seeds – inadequately stored seeds can reduce their viability. To check if they're still viable, take 10 seeds from the packets and fold them into a damp kitchen towel. Place in a sandwich bag and pop it somewhere warm for a week, making sure the kitchen towel doesn't dry out.

If you think the seeds may have been eaten, try protecting trays with propagator lids until germination, or place them on a high shelf away from mice, voles and slugs.

thin, tall stem / few leaves

INSUFFICIENT LIGHT AND HAS GONE 'LEGGY'

Seedlings need plenty of light to grow strong. Once germinated, you need to put your seedlings in a position with full light, such as a greenhouse or conservatory. A position with less light, such as a windowsill, means they'll keep searching out light by stretching upwards instead of focussing their energy on building a strong root system, and strong stem and leaf canopy. I call these stretched seedlings 'leggy'. Place your seedling in full light in a conservatory, polytunnel, cold frame or greenhouse.

shrivelling, leaves crisping at the edges, browning, curling leaves

UNDERWATERING

When you have visibly dry soil, and your seedlings are struggling, they're likely suffering from underwatering. Regularly check on them, and on particularly hot days you might need to water a couple of times. Water from underneath to ensure the whole cell of compost gets moistened.

spotted, crispy, wilted, bleached and scorched leaves

SUNBURN

Too much direct sunshine on a hot day, or watering your seedlings when the sun is at its highest and strongest, can cause sunburn. Try sunshades in your growing space and water in the morning and evening only.

spots on leaves

INSECT DAMAGE

Healthy seedlings are less susceptible to insect damage. If your seedlings have been hit by the bugs, try more warmth and better circulation.

eaten leaves

Search for the culprit – usually slugs or mice. Slugs love to live on the underside of seed trays. Remove the culprits. Try nematodes to keep your growing areas slug-free. Place seed trays where mice can't climb to.

brown pustules

RUST DISEASE

Rust disease can happen when the leaves remain wet when watering. Water from underneath to avoid this. If you see rust, get rid of seedlings and compost and properly clean the tray or pot.

need to feed
and how to feed

You shouldn't need to feed your seedlings unless you're over-wintering them, they're getting quite sizeable and are beginning to sulk. The bigger a seedling gets, the more nutrients they need, and when they're stuck in little pots they may use up all available nutrients.

- *Potting on allows seedlings a little more space to grow, but also gives fresh nutrients from the added compost*

- *If leaves begin to yellow, the seedlings may be telling you that they're hungry*

- *Pot them on, and give them a boost by adding a little seaweed liquid fertilizer or comfrey tea to your water tray when you water them into their new pots. Feed again weekly until planting out*

- *Check the recommended dose for bought-in fertilizer*

- *Water to homemade comfrey tea ratio – 1:10*

how to prick out

Prick out when the seedling is large enough to handle; this is usually when the leaf is close in size to the nail on your little finger.

1. Lever out the seedlings carefully using something pointy to get into the soil without breaking their roots, such as a widger or a pen.

2. Hold the seedling by the leaf – the reason for this is if you're going to damage the seedling, the leaf is of lesser importance than the root or the stem.

3. Make a little hole in the compost of your seed cell or pot.

4. Dangle the root into the hole and nestle it in so the leaves are sitting close to the soil surface.

5. Backfill the rest of the hole with compost.

6. Gently firm the compost around the seedling.

7. Water in to ensure any air pockets collapse and the roots have good contact with the soil.

how to pot on

A seedling is ready to be potted on when the roots have filled the cell.

A good way of telling is if you can see the roots growing through the bottom of the drainage holes. Then make sure they're ready by levering a seedling and its root ball out. If the roots have reached the bottom of the cell or pot but there's still plenty of compost without roots in yet, then leave it to keep on growing where it is. If the seedling has a good root system that fills the cell or pot, then it's time to pot on.

1. *Fill the next pot size up with multi-purpose compost.*

2. *Dib a hole in the surface big enough to accommodate your seedling and its whole root ball.*

3. *Place your seedling in and fill in with compost.*

4. *Water in to collapse any air pockets.*

5. *Fill in with a little extra compost if required.*

pinching out

Many flower varieties benefit from a pinch. There are growth hormones in the main stem and when you pinch out the main growing tip, the growth hormone strength will be diverted to the side shoots. This means bushier plants with more shoots, and therefore, more stems and more flowers.

A good general rule of when to pinch is when the seedling is between 20 cm (8 in) and 30 cm (12 in) tall, or when it has at least 3–5 sets of true leaves. It's best to pinch in active growth, so avoid pinching in winter low-light dormancy. You want to make sure that the leaves are big enough to allow good photosynthesis to still occur after pinching.

Bear in mind that pinching will hold back the flowering time a little, but it's worth it for all the extra stems you'll get from it.

1. *Choose to pinch either the second or third set of true leaves.*

2. *Using your thumb and forefinger, or a clean pair of snips, pinch out the stem just above a set of leaves where there will be sideshoots budding.*

3. *Be careful not to damage the stem or leaves below the pinch.*

4. *Don't pinch stocks or single-stemmed sunflowers, as they don't branch and you'll end up with no flower.*

hardening off

Introduce stresses gradually and one at a time when hardening off your seedlings. Leave a day or two at least between introducing a new stage of hardening off.

1. If starting your seeds in the house, move from indoors to a heat mat in a greenhouse.
2. Move off the heat mat in the greenhouse.
3. Move trays outside during the day (make sure to choose a protected spot, not too exposed to wind and sun stressors).
4. Leave trays outside day and night (make sure there are no frosts as the roots will be particularly vulnerable to frosts if still in trays).
5. Plant out in the ground.

when and how to plant out

Hardier plants can be planted out a little before the last frosts. Tender and young plants must be planted out once the danger of frosts has passed.

1. Prepare your seed beds with a layer of compost (you can do this back in autumn or in spring before planting).
2. Once the plants have been properly hardened off, bring them out to plant.
3. Rake the top of the bed until it's flat and there are no big lumps on the surface.
4. If using irrigation, lay your drip line and secure with pegs.
5. Mark out the desired spacing for the variety you're planting out.
6. Using a trowel, make a hole a little bigger than the size of pot you're planting out.
7. Remove your young plant from the pot (or cell tray).
8. Place it in the hole and backfill with compost.
9. Firm in the compost around the plant.
10. Water to ensure any air pockets collapse (this will help roots find compost to grow into, rather than air).

watering and irrigation

- *Rainwater is best for more established plants and plants outside*
- *Mains water is best for seeds under cover*

If using mains water for irrigating your outdoor plants, you must use managed-water practices. This means having a water tank, butt or an Immediate Bulk Container (IBC) to store your mains water so you can see and control how much you're actually using (even better if you can collect rainwater from a gutter into your tank, butt or IBC).

irrigation

There are a handful of useful irrigation parts that can help you build the perfect irrigation system. You can find them online, or even better, find your local irrigation specialist who might be able to offer advice for your specific conditions.

PUMP

This helps the pressure of the water to reach the end of the irrigation evenly.

FEEDER PIPES

The pipes that move the water to your beds – they have no little holes. Feeder pipe tends to be more robust and can be laid in shallow ditches in the ground.

DRIP TAPE OR DRIP LINE

The pipes for your beds, which have little holes at intervals so the water drips out to your seedlings. Drip tape is cheaper, but I find it breaks easily and disintegrates after a season or two. For longevity and less maintenance, opt for drip line over tape.

PEGS

These hold the pipes in place on your beds.

JOINER

This joins two pipes together, perfect for fixing a leak or joining two pieces of pipe that are too short.

VALVE JUNCTION

A valve junction can open and close a pipe. Great at the top of a bed so you can manually turn on or off as you need.

TEE JUNCTION

To connect a feeder pipe and drip line.

ELBOW JUNCTION

For a corner connecting a feeder pipe and a drip line.

STOP END

For the pipe end to stop the water flow.

SOLENOID VALVE

An electrical component for creating multi-zones for separate watering.

plant support

As plants grow, many will need support, either against the wind or from the weight of their own newly-grown, voluptuous flower heads. It's important to create this infrastructure before they need it, because by the time the season is underway it's easy to be too busy or forgetful, so it's best to get done as the beds get made.

STAKING

If you're growing with a wider spacing, use a stake to tie in each individual plant. Use a mallet to get a stake next to the plant, with at least 30 cm (1 ft) in the ground for maximum strength.

CORRALING

Using stakes around 1.5 m (5 ft) in length, use a mallet to place them roughly every 60 cm (2 ft) around a bed with at least 1.2 m (4 ft) left above ground. Corral the entire bed with strong twine at two different heights. You can zigzag the twine across the beds from post to post, too, adding an extra layer of support for stems.

NETTING

Using stakes around 1.5 m (5 ft) in length, use a mallet to place them roughly every 60 cm (2 ft) around a bed with at least 1.2 m (4 ft) left above ground. For the more fragile stemmed plants, such as scabious, cosmos and phlox, I tie netting across the stakes for them to grow up through, and this helps them to grow tall and strong.

TRELLIS AND PYRAMID

For climbers, you'll need a structure to climb. Get a taller stake, around 2 m (6½ ft) in length, and place it in a hole at least 50 cm (20 in) deep, compacting the soil around the stake to make sure it's in securely. You can have a line of these stakes and stretch netting between them for your plants to climb.

Alternatively, create a pyramid structure using 5–6 stakes. Make sure at least 30 cm (1 ft) of each stake is in the ground. Pull them together to meet at the top, and secure with strong twine. Using strong twine, gently and securely tie the stalks of your plants to the stakes. Leave a little space between the twine and the plant – although the stems need to be well supported, it's wise not to tie too tightly – leave a little room for the stem to grow in diameter without being damaged by the twine. Keep tying in as they grow.

Clockwise from top left: pea 'Spring Blush'; sweet pea 'Leominster Boy', Frances Kate 'Janey' and 'Suzy z'; sweet pea 'Leominster Boy', Frances Kate 'Janey' and 'Suzy z'; calendula 'Orange Flash' and Orlaya.

harvesting flowers

The moment we've all been working towards – the harvests. The one main tip for harvesting is to do it in the evening or first thing in the morning once the dew has dried. In the evening, the plants have stored carbohydrates from the day, which offers a food reserve. In the morning transpiration (losing water through small openings called stomata in their leaves) in the plant is low, which affects the turgidity of the stem. Cutting them when they're naturally losing less water is best. Then, placing them immediately into a bucket of water to start conditioning will help them recover from harvest and stay hydrated. Choose to cut from only healthy plants.

• *Cut stems with clean, sharp and sanitized secateurs straight into clean buckets of water*

• *Harvest when the transpiration of the plants is at its lowest at dawn and dusk. Remove any excess leaves, paying special attention to removing the leaves that will sit under the waterline*

• *Let the flowers drink somewhere cool and dark – a garden shed is ideal, for at least 6 hours (or overnight) before working with them*

(For more information on harvesting cut flowers, see The Grower's Guide: Floristry)

seasonal favourites

With a little space under cover, you can extend your growing season of annuals and biennials to flower earlier in late spring.

LATE SPRING

Cerinthe, sweet peas, *Orlaya*, corncockles, *Silene*, red campion, *Phacelia*, honesty, sweet rocket, foxgloves, *Briza maxima*, stocks

EARLY SUMMER

Violas, snapdragons, larkspur, nigella, *Ammi*, poppies, sweet William, cornflowers, *Malope*, lavatera, scabious, *Cynoglossum*, statice

LATE SUMMER

Cosmos, orach, zinnias, *Daucus*, Chinese asters, *Panicum*, nasturtiums, phlox, dill, *Nicotiana*, *Gomphrena*, bells of Ireland, *Ammi visnaga*

EARLY AUTUMN

Rudbeckia, Amaranthus, Cobaea

seed saving: collecting and storing seed

HARVESTING

Generally, seeds are ripe for harvesting when the seed pod turns from green to brown. The very best quality seeds are from the first flowers to go to seed. If the whole plant is harvested, you can hang it to dry and ripen further under cover in a polytunnel – or for smaller seed heads, lay them out on paper indoors. If laid out, keep turning so the seeds dry evenly and avoid rot.

THRESHING

Once dry, the seed will have to be separated from the mother plant material. You can do this by breaking up the plant material, crushing it in a bucket or rubbing it out in your hands while wearing rubbing gloves. This is called threshing.

WINNOWING

You'll be left with small fragments of the mother plant, called chaff. To sort the seeds from the chaff you can use wind. Wait for a windy day and pass them from one bucket to another, allowing the wind to carry the chaff away until the seeds are as clean as you'd like. This process is called winnowing. If you're impatient for wind, try a fan!

STORING SEEDS

Temperature Can Affect Seed Viability. Seeds are highly sensitive to temperature variations, and even minor fluctuations can significantly impact their germination rates and overall development. Seeds stored in hot temperatures for extended periods risk damage to the embryo and reduce the viability of germination. Seeds need to be kept cool and dry to ensure their quality. A stable environment is key.

botanical names

COMMON NAME	BOTANICAL NAME	COMMON NAME	BOTANICAL NAME
Amaranth	*Amaranthus*	Guernsey Lily	*Nerine*
Angelica	*Angelica*	Hellebore	*Helleborus*
Bellflower	*Campanula*	Hollyhock	*Alcea*
Bells of Ireland	*Moluccella laevis*	Honesty	*Lunaria*
Bergamot	*Monarda*	Honeywort	*Cerinthe*
Bishop's Flower	*Ammi*	Hound's Tongue	*Cynoglossum*
Black-eyed Susan	*Rudbeckia*	Icelandic Poppy	*Papaver nudicaule*
Bleeding Heart	*Dicentra*	Jacob's Ladder	*Polemonium*
Boneset	*Eupatorium*	Jerusalem Sage	*Phlomis*
Burnet	*Sanguisorba*	Khella	*Ammi visnaga*
Campion	*Silene*	Knotweed	*Persicaria*
Carnation	*Dianthus*	Lace Flower	*Orlaya*
Carrot	*Daucus carota*	Lady's Mantle	*Alchemilla mollis*
Catnip	*Nepeta*	Larkspur	*Delphinium*
Chinese aster	*Callistephus chinensis*	Love-in-the-Mist	*Nigella*
Chrysanthemum	*Chrysanthemum*	Lupin	*Lupinus*
Columbine	*Aquilegia*	Mallow	*Malope*
Comfrey	*Symphytum*	Marigold	*Tagetes*
Coneflower	*Echinacea*	Masterwort	*Astrantia*
Corncockle	*Agrostemma githago*	Meadow Rue	*Thalictrum*
Cornflower	*Centaurea cyanus*	Michaelmas Daisy	*Aster*
Cosmos	*Cosmos*	Mullein	*Verbascum*
Cup and Saucer Vine	*Cobaea*	Nasturtium	*Tropaeolum*
Daffodil	*Narcissus*	Orach	*Atriplex hortensis*
Dahlia	*Dahlia*	Oregano	*Origanum*
Dame's Rocket	*Hesperis*	Oxeye Daisy	*Leucanthemum*
Dill	*Anethum graveolens*	Panicgrass	*Panicum*
False Goat's Beard	*Astilbe*	Pansy	*Viola*
Foxglove	*Digitalis*	Peony	*Paeonia*
Fringecup	*Tellima*	Phacelia	*Phacelia*
Gaura	*Oenothera lindheimeri*	Phlox	*Phlox*
Geranium	*Pelargonium*	Poppy	*Papaver*
Globe Amaranth	*Gomphrena*	Pot Marigold	*Calendula*
Goat's Beard	*Aruncus*	Primrose	*Primula*
Great Quaking-Grass	*Briza maxima*	Red Campion	*Silene*

COMMON NAME	BOTANICAL NAME
Rose	*Rosa*
Russian Sage	*Perovskia*
Sage	*Salvia*
Scabious	*Scabiosa*
Sea Holly	*Eryngium*
Snapdragon	*Antirrhinum*
Speedwell	*Veronica*
Statice	*Limonium*
Stock	*Matthiola*
Stonecrop	*Sedum*
Strawflower	*Xerochrysum bracteatum*
Sunflower	*Helianthus*
Sweet Pea	*Lathyrus odoratus*
Sweet Rocket	*Hesperis*
Sweet William	*Dianthus barbatus*
Thistle	*Cirsium*
Tickseed	*Coreopsis*
Tobacco Plant	*Nicotiana*
Tree Mallow	*Lavatera*
Tulip	*Tulipa*
Verbena	*Verbena bonariensis*
Violet	*Viola*
Wallflower	*Erysimum*
Wood Avens	*Geum*
Woolflower	*Celosia*
Yarrow	*Achillea*
Zinnia	*Zinnia*

acknowledgements

Thanks to Molly Wansell, agent and dear friend who has weathered many dead ends with me. Thanks for coming down this garden path with me, it's been a dream. Thanks to Jan Wansell for sowing the seed of the idea of books – I'm so glad you did. Thanks to my Quadrille team, it's always a pleasure to create with you. Thanks to Éva, the kindest talent out there. Your pictures make everything special. Thanks to Paris for being the fortifying and strengthening force that you are. A miracle that we have spun into each others lives, everything is more beautiful and fun with you by my side. Thanks to Ted, the loveliest partner, and all you do for us. Thanks to Rex for being the strongest, funniest and gentlest soul, I can't wait to watch you grow. And thank you to everyone who has helped Rex and I heal through those difficult times – to the ones who have held him close by and let me find myself again amongst the flowers.

Managing Director Sarah Lavelle
Senior Commissioning Editor Harriet Butt
Editorial Assistant Ellie Spence
Senior Designer Gemma Hayden
Photographer Éva Németh
Illustrations Milli Proust
Head of Production Stephen Lang
Senior Production Controller Sabeena Atchia

Published in 2024 by Quadrille,
an imprint of Hardie Grant Publishing

Quadrille
52–54 Southwark Street
London SE1 1UN
quadrille.com

Cataloguing in Publication Data:
a catalogue record for this book is
available from the British Library

Text, illustrations and floral
   designs © Milli Proust 2024
Photography © Éva Németh 2024
Design and layout © Quadrille 2024

ISBN 978 1 83783 180 7
Printed in China using soy inks

MIX
Paper | Supporting
responsible forestry
FSC™ C020056